Summer
Adventures

Written by Catherine Saunders

LONDON, NEW YORK, MUNICH,
MELBOURNE and DELHI

DK LONDON
Editor Lisa Stock
Senior Editor Victoria Taylor
Senior Designer Lisa Sodeau
Pre-Production Producer Siu Yin Chan
Producer Louise Daly
Managing Editor Elizabeth Dowsett
Design Manager Nathan Martin
Publishing Manager Julie Ferris
Art Director Ron Stobbart
Publishing Director Simon Beecroft

DK DELHI
Assistant Editor Gaurav Joshi
Senior Editor Garima Sharma
Assistant Art Editor Suzena Sengupta
Deputy Managing Art Editor Neha Ahuja
DTP Designer Umesh Singh Rawat
Senior DTP Designer Jagtar Singh
Pre-Production Manager Sunil Sharma

Reading Consultant
Maureen Fernandes

First published in Great Britain in 2014 by
Dorling Kindersley Limited
80 Strand, London, WC2R 0RL

10 9 8 7 6 5 4 3 2 1
001–196560–Jan/14

Page design copyright © 2014 Dorling Kindersley Limited
LEGO, the LEGO logo, the Brick and the Knob configurations
are trademarks of the LEGO Group.
© 2014 The LEGO Group
Produced by Dorling Kindersley under licence from the LEGO Group.

A CIP catalogue record for this book is
available from the British Library.

ISBN: 978-1-40934-681-4

Colour reproduction by Alta Image
Printed and bound in China by South China

Discover more at
www.dk.com
www.LEGO.com

Contents

4   Summer's Here!

6   What's Up, Girls?

8   Up, Up and Away!

12   Writing Adventures

14   Dear Ella

16   Horsing Around

18   Welcome to Riding Camp

20   Summer Job

22   We Can Do It!

24   Time to Relax

26   Emma's Big Splash!

28   Indoor Adventures

30   Emma's Mood Board

32   Makeover Time

34   Helping Out

36   Summer Show

38   Heartlake City News

40   Find the Beat

42   Outdoor Adventures

44   Take a Trip

50   A Day in the Country

52   Inventing Adventures

54   Secret Place

56   Amazing Adventures

58   Quiz

60   Glossary

61   Index

62   Guide for Parents

Summer's Here!

It is summertime in Heartlake City. With no school for a few weeks, Mia, Olivia, Stephanie, Andrea and Emma can enjoy the sunshine. They have some great ideas for summer fun.

Turn the page to find out what each girl is up to over the summer and, most importantly, what they will be doing together.

There is something exciting to suit everyone, so come and join the girls on their fantastic summer adventures.

What's Up, Girls?

Stephanie

Hi everyone! I'm so excited, the holidays are here.

Did I tell you I'm going to fly my seaplane? I'll be able to see the city from the sky!

Andrea

Guess who's working at the City Park Café? Me! I want to save up enough over the summer for those singing classes…

Emma

Well, when you finish work, Andrea, you can join us all in my splash pool!

That sounds like fun, Emma. Did you know I'm training my puppy, Charlie, for a dog show?

Mia

Olivia

That's amazing, Mia! I plan to spend most of my time at the beach.

Up, Up and Away!

Stephanie thinks the best place
to have a summer adventure is
in the sky.

She has a special type of plane
that can take off and land on water.
It is called a seaplane.

Stephanie has been taking flying lessons at the Heartlake Flying Club for a few months. She is a natural!

At last, Stephanie is qualified to fly her seaplane all by herself. She is ready for take off on her first solo flight!

After a smooth take off, Stephanie is up, up and away! The weather is perfect and Stephanie can see what her friends are doing.

Look! There is Mia. She is at the stables grooming her horse, Bella. Is that Emma? Yes, she is shopping on Main Street.

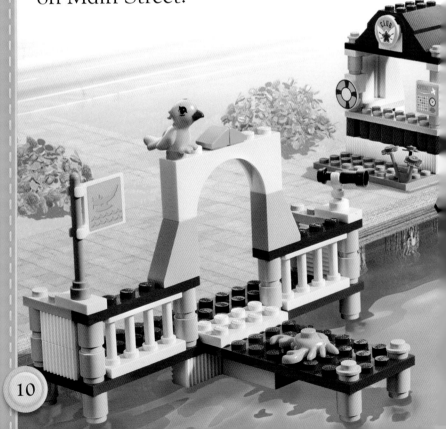

It looks like Olivia is building something amazing in her garden.

Stephanie knows just where to find Andrea: there she is, hard at work in the City Park Café. After a great trip, Stephanie heads back to make a perfect landing.

Writing Adventures

Stephanie is very sociable and she has many friends all over the world. She is super organised and keeps in touch with all of them.

Stephanie loves to write long letters to her pen pals. She has even designed her own notepaper.

Today, Stephanie is posting a letter to her pen friend Ella. They write to each other every week and see each other every summer holiday.

21, Floral Street,
Heartlake City

4th August

Dear Ella,

It's summertime, so I have no school for the next few weeks.
Summer holidays are so much fun! Finally, we can meet up
again. We have so much to catch up on!

Do you remember my friend Emma? Well, Emma and I are
going to riding camp this summer. Would you like to come?

We can learn how to ride horses, as well as how to groom and
feed them. There's also a classroom at the camp where we can
learn all about horses. I hope you can come!

Love,
Stephanie

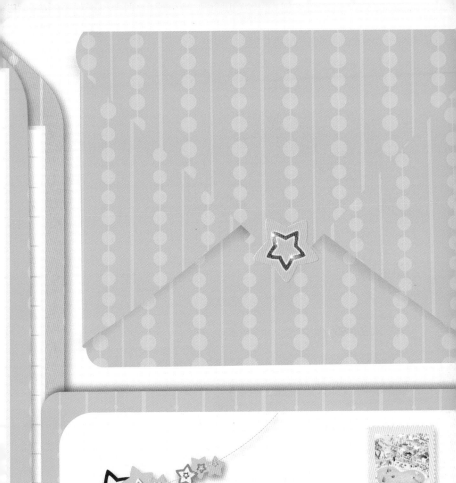

Ella

75, Baker's Street,

Paradisa Town

Horsing Around

During the summer, Stephanie, Emma and Mia love spending time with their favourite animals – horses. Mia spends as much time as possible at the stables with her horse, Bella.

This summer, Stephanie and
Emma are going to riding camp,
with Stephanie's friend Ella. In the
morning, their trainer, Theresa,
teaches them how to care for horses.
In the afternoon, they practise riding
in the training paddock. At the end
of the day, the girls groom and feed
the horses and then put them safely
in their stables.

Welcome to
Riding Camp!

Wheelbarrow

Oscar

Riding helmet

Theresa,
the trainer

Grooming
brush

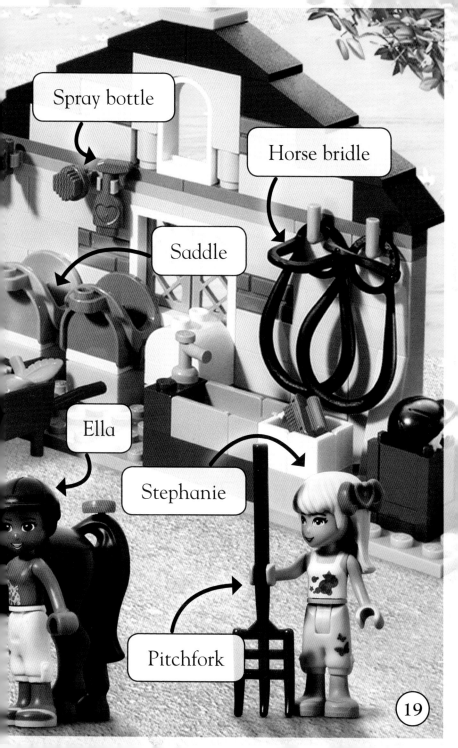

Spray bottle

Horse bridle

Saddle

Ella

Stephanie

Pitchfork

19

Summer Job

Andrea is busy working this summer.
She is a waitress at the City Park Café.
It is a lot of hard work, but Andrea
does not mind. She is saving up
for extra singing lessons.

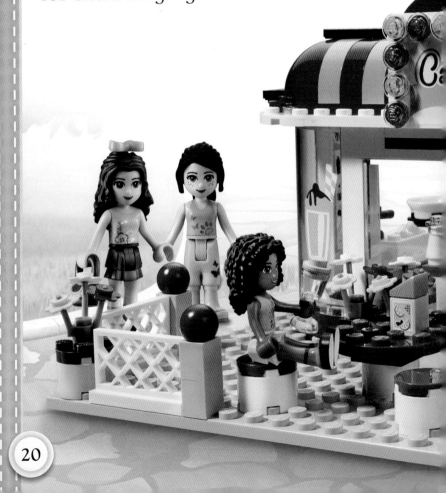

Working in the café also gives Andrea the chance to practise her singing. Whether she is mopping, washing up or just putting her feet up, Andrea is happy to entertain the customers with a song!

I love music! And I enjoy writing my own songs, too.

We Can Do It!

Can you see the stars are in my eyes? And I feel so good today!

Friends are like the stars across my sky, shining bright in everyway.

There is a world full of magic that I want to build with you.

Be a part of all my friends
and the fun just never ends.

(Chorus) We can do it!
Friends are here to stay
We can dream a whole new way.

(Chorus) We can do it!
Girls to show the way
So build the world with me today...

Time to Relax

For Emma, summer is about
relaxing and taking it easy
after working so hard at school.
Her friends agree and they like to
make time to just
chill out together.

Emma's summer house is right by the beach. It is the perfect place for Emma, Mia, Stephanie, Olivia and Andrea to hang out. The girls meet up at the summer house to sunbathe, and catch up on each other's summer adventures.

Welcome, Emma!

Inbox 15

Sent	125
Drafts	1

New Message

Send

Save

Delete

To: Andrea, Stephanie, Mia, Olivia

From: Emma

Subject: My Pool Party!   1 Attachment 📎

Emma's Big Splash!

It's time to enjoy the sun!

Please come to a party in my splash pool.

There will be lemonade and ice cream
sundaes to help us beat the heat!

Tuesday at 4pm

*At my summer house
(right by the beach!)*

Don't forget to bring your flip-flops,
swimming costumes and
lots of suntan lotion!

Indoor Adventures

During the summer, Emma tries to spend as much time as possible in her studio.

Emma wants to be a fashion designer and is working on her own fashion collection.

Emma has so many great ideas! She uses the internet to research styles and fabrics, then she draws her designs and pins them up on her mood board.

Emma takes fashion very seriously. She keeps telling her friends that accessories can make or break an outfit.

A blue top and pink skirt are a perfect match. The matching shoes look good, too.

My favourite colours!

My Mood Board
by Emma

This purple top goes well with my white trousers, and I love my black riding boots.

A floral top with a pink skirt and white shoes is perfect for a summery look!

Purple and pink are so in season!

Handbags can make an ordinary
outfit into a fabulous one.
I can't decide which is
my favourite!

I love accessorising my outfits with
colourful bows and pretty bags.

Makeover Time

Emma wants a new look this summer. She goes to the Butterfly Beauty Shop and asks Sarah for something fabulous!

Sarah knows just what to do to give Emma her look. Now all Emma needs to complete the effect is a cute hair accessory and the perfect shade of lipstick.

Emma cannot decide which lipstick will look best. Fortunately, Mia is passing by the Beauty Shop and is happy to help Emma out. Emma's new look is fabulous!

Helping Out

Mia is crazy about all animals, not just horses. During the summer, she is a volunteer helper with the Heartlake City vet, Sophie.

Mia feeds the animals, cleans their cages, exercises them and even talks to them if they are scared or hurt.

Mia likes the animals and they seem to like her, too.

Mia would like to be a vet one day. She wants to learn as much as possible from Sophie.

Summer Show

Mia has a busy summer, but she makes sure that her pets have fun, too. She enters her puppy, Charlie, into the annual Heartlake City Dog Show.

Mia is determined that Charlie will win the prize for the Most Agile Puppy.

Mia puts in a lot of hard work and practice to train Charlie. Luckily, Mia is a talented animal trainer and Charlie is very clever.

Cute Puppy Steals the Show!

Heartlake City Correspondent

Picture Credit: Heartlake City News

The annual Heartlake City Dog Show, held yesterday, was a great success. Dogs of all shapes and sizes performed in the competition. But it was one very cute puppy, Charlie, that won over the judges.

Charlie's owner, Mia, had taught him some amazing tricks.

He performed a spectacular balancing act on a seesaw.

Nobody was surprised when Charlie was declared the winner. He won the prize for Most Agile Puppy.

Another puppy, Scarlett, who belongs to Mia's friend Olivia, took second place in the same category.

Find the Beat

Mia wants to learn a new skill this summer, so she is teaching herself to play the drums. She plans to play her cool set of drums every day in her bedroom.

Mia practises by turning the radio up high and keeping the beat to her favourite songs. She is getting pretty good at it and is thinking about starting her own rock group.

Outdoor Adventures

The weather is always good
in Heartlake City and both
Mia and Olivia like to have
exciting outdoor adventures.

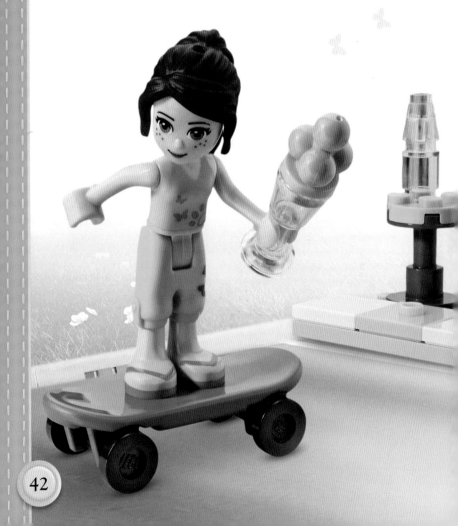

Mia loves skateboarding and spends a lot of time at the City Park practising jumps and tricks. She thinks she will soon be ready to take part in a local skateboarding competition.

Olivia prefers speedboats to skateboards. She has learnt to drive her parents' speedboat, and loves taking it out on the ocean.

Take a Trip

Olivia thinks summer is the perfect time to explore the countryside in her stylish pink camper van. It has a TV and enough space for two people to sleep in it.

Olivia knows just who she wants to share this summer adventure with – her friend Nicole.

Nicole thinks the trip sounds like fun! The two girls pack their bags and load their bikes and surfboards into the trailer. It is time to set off on their summer adventure!

Olivia finds a quiet spot to park
the camper van, and the two friends
set off on a bike ride.

It is a great way to catch up.
They talk about everything that
has happened since they last met.

Nicole has a new pet cat and has been taking cookery lessons.

Olivia tells Nicole about her friends Mia, Stephanie, Andrea and Emma. Nicole thinks they sound like a lot of fun and would like to meet them all one day.

After a great night's sleep in the camper van, Olivia and Nicole drive down to the beach. The girls prepare a delicious picnic and then head down to the ocean with their surfboards.

Nicole has never been surfing before, so Olivia gives her a lesson. Soon Nicole is an expert surfer.

It has been a tiring day. In the evening, the girls relax in the van, playing games and watching TV. What a wonderful summer adventure!

A Day in the Country

Olivia and I decided to explore the
countryside around Heartlake City
– it was so much fun!

*Olivia's van is the best way to
get around during the summer!*

We saw cows and horses. It was such a lovely sunny day that I just had to take lots of pictures!

Lunchtime! I grilled some chicken while Olivia topped up her tan!

This scrapbook belongs to ...Nicole......

Inventing Adventures

Olivia is a budding inventor.
She experiments with new ideas
and designs amazing gadgets in
her own workshop.

This summer she
has created her most
ambitious invention
yet – a robot!
His name is Zobo.

Olivia thinks Zobo is really cool.
She can make him fetch things
using her remote control pad.
Zobo is really easy to look after,
too. He just needs to be oiled
regularly so he does not go rusty.

Secret Place

Olivia believes that she does not have to travel far for the best summer adventures. That is because she and her friends have an amazing treehouse, which no one else knows about. Olivia found the treehouse near her new house when she moved to Heartlake City, and the girls worked hard together to fix it up.

The treehouse is the perfect meeting place. The girls can hang out, share their secrets and plan their next adventure.

Amazing Adventures

Summer is nearly over but Emma, Stephanie, Andrea, Mia and Olivia have time for one last barbecue.

The girls have had lots of fantastic summer adventures – some relaxing, some thrilling and some downright hard work!

However, they all know what the most important part of any summer adventure is – sharing it with your best friends.

Friends can make a good summer, a fabulous summer. Now it is your turn: how will you spend your summer?

Quiz

1. What kind of a plane does Stephanie fly?

2. Who is Stephanie's pen pal?

3. Where does Andrea work?

4. What is the name of Andrea's song?

5. Where is Emma's summer house?

6. Where does Emma go to get a makeover?

7. What is the name of Mia's horse?

8. What is Mia teaching herself to do?

9. What is Olivia's robot's name?

10. Who does Olivia go on holiday with in her camper van?

Answers on
page 61

Glossary

accessories
items used to complement an outfit, for example, a bag or jewellery

agile
ability to move quickly and easily

bridle
headgear for horses

camper van
holiday vehicle used for transportation and also for sleeping in

correspondent
person who writes for a newspaper on special topics

flightpath
route that an aircraft takes when flying

makeover
changing your appearance

mood board
board used to display colour samples, ideas, textures, fabrics, etc.

paddock
small field where horses are exercised

sociable
someone friendly who loves being with people

Index

beach 7, 25, 27, 48

bikes 45

Butterfly Beauty Shop
  32, 33

camper van 44, 46, 48

Charlie 7, 36, 37, 39

City Park Café 6, 11, 20

drums 40

fashion designer 29

Heartlake City 4, 14,
  38–39, 42, 50, 54

Heartlake City Vet 34

holidays 6, 13, 14

horses 14, 16–17, 34, 51

notebook 22

lemonade 27

lessons 9, 20, 47, 48

pen pals 12

picnic 48

radio 41

riding camp 14, 17,
  18–19

seaplane 6, 8, 9

skateboarding 43

songs 22, 41

splash pool 7, 27

stables 10, 16, 17

surfboards 45, 48

trailer 45

TV 44, 49

Answers to the quiz on pages 58 and 59:
1. A seaplane 2. Ella 3. At the City Park Café
4. *We Can Do It* 5. By the beach 6. To the
Butterfly Beauty Shop 7. Bella 8. To play
the drums 9. Zobo 10. Nicole

Guide for Parents

DK Reads is a three-level reading series for children, developing the habit of reading widely for both pleasure and information. These books have an exciting running text interspersed with a range of reading genres to suit your child's reading ability, as required by the school curriculum. Each book is designed to develop your child's reading skills, fluency, grammar awareness and comprehension in order to build confidence and engagement when reading.

Ready for a *Starting to Read Alone* book
YOUR CHILD SHOULD
- be able to read most words without needing to stop and break them down into sound parts.
- read smoothly, in phrases and with expression. By this level, your child will be mostly reading silently.
- self-correct when a word or sentence doesn't sound right.

A Valuable and Shared Reading Experience

For some children, text reading, particularly non-fiction, requires much effort but adult participation can make this both fun and easier. So here are a few tips on how to use this book with your child.

TIP 1: Check out the contents together before your child begins:
- Invite your child to check the blurb, contents page and layout of the book and comment on it.
- Ask your child to make predictions about the story.
- Chat about the information your child might want to find out.

TIP 2: Encourage fluent and flexible reading:

- Support your child to read in fluent, expressive phrases, making full use of punctuation and thinking about the meaning. Demonstrate this if necessary.
- Encourage your child to slow down and check information where appropriate.

Reading aloud is a way of communicating, just like talking and keeping a voice varied draws in the listener.

TIP 3: Indicators that your child is reading for meaning:

- Your child will be responding to the text if he/she is self-correcting and varying his/her voice.
- Your child will want to chat about what he/she is reading or is eager to turn the page to find out what will happen next.

TIP 4: Praise, share and chat:

- The factual pages tend to be more difficult than the story pages, and are designed to be shared with your child.
- Encourage your child to recall specific details after each chapter.
- Provide opportunities for your child to pick out interesting words and discuss what they mean.
- Discuss how the author captures the reader's interest, or how effective the non-fiction layouts are.
- Ask questions about the text. These help to develop comprehension skills and awareness of the language used.

A FEW ADDITIONAL TIPS

- Read to your child regularly to demonstrate fluency, phrasing and expression; to find out or check information; and for sharing enjoyment.
- Encourage your child to reread favourite texts to increase reading confidence and fluency.
- Check that your child is reading a range of different types of text, such as poems, jokes or instructions.

Here are some other DK Reads you might enjoy.

Starting to Read Alone

The Great Panda Tale
Join the excitement at the zoo as the staff prepare
to welcome a new panda baby.

Terrors of the Deep
Marine biologists Dom and Jake take their
deep-sea submersible down into the deepest, darkest
ocean trenches in the world.

Pony Club
Emma is so excited – she is going to horse-riding
camp with her older sister!

Reading Alone

Star Wars™: Jedi Battles
Join the Jedi on their epic adventures and exciting battles.
Meet brave Jedi Knights who fight for justice across the galaxy.

Star Wars™: Sith Wars
Meet the Sith Lords who are trying to take over the galaxy.
Discover their evil plans and deadly armies.